JAN   2007

HOW DO BIRDS FLY?

MELISSA STEWART

 **Marshall Cavendish**
Benchmark
New York

Marshall Cavendish Benchmark
99 White Plains Road
Tarrytown, New York 10591-9001
www.marshallcavendish.us

All Web sites were available and accurate when this book was sent to press.

Editor: D. Sanders
Editorial Director: Michelle Bisson
Art Director: Anahid Hamparian
Series Designer: Alex Ferrari

Library of Congress Cataloging-in-Publication Data

Stewart, Melissa.
How do birds fly? / by Melissa Stewart.
p. cm. — (Tell me why, tell me how)
Summary: "An examination of the phenomena and scientific principles behind
bird flight"—Provided by publisher.
Includes bibliographical references.
ISBN-13: 978-0-7614-2110-8 (alk. paper)
ISBN-10: 0-7614-2110-6 (alk. paper)
1. Birds—Flight—Juvenile literature. I. Title. II. Series.

QL698.7S84 2006
598.15'7—dc22

2005017262

Photo research by Candlepants Incorporated

Cover photo: Gusto Productions/Photo Researchers Inc.

The photographs in this book are used by permission and through the courtesy of: *U.S .Fish & Wildlife Services:*
Wyman Meinzer, 1; David Hall, 8; Steve Maslowski, 24. *Photo Researchers Inc.:* Chris Butler, 5; Millard H. Sharp,
7; Hugh Turvey, 9; Oliver Meckes/Nicole Ottawa, 13; Larry West, 22; Gerald C. Kelly, 26. *Minden Pictures:* Flip
DeNooyer/Foto Natura, 6; Franz Lanting, 10; Andre Wieringa/Foto Natura, 14; Michael & Patricia Fogden, 19.
SuperStock: age fotostock, 4, 12, 18; M. Cohen, 16. *S. Nielsen/UNEP/Still Pictures/Peter Arnold Inc.:* 15. *Keran
Su/Corbis:* 25.

Printed in Malaysia
1 3 5 6 4 2

CONTENTS

Scientists believe that birds
are related to dinosaurs.

Why Birds Fly

Scientists believe that birds **evolved** from dinosaurs about 150 million years ago. The first birds were about the size of crows. They were like their **reptile** relatives in many ways, but with a few important differences. The earliest birds had wings with feathers. They could probably fly—though not very far and not very well.

This drawing shows an artist's idea of what the earliest birds might have looked like.

Over time, birds have become expert fliers. Their bodies have changed in ways that make them able to soar through the air. Being able to fly allows birds to live almost anywhere in the world. They can be found on the frozen tundra and in tropical rain forests. They also live in farmers' fields and in crowded cities.

These long-eared owl chicks live in a forest in Europe.

If this bluebird could not fly, it would not have been able to capture its meal.

No matter where a bird lives, flying helps it find food and escape danger. Flying also allows birds to travel long distances. Many birds **migrate,** or fly to far-off places, twice each year. In the autumn, migrating birds fly to warmer **habitats** that have plenty of food. When spring arrives, the birds return to cooler places to feed and raise their young.

Now I Know!

Scientists believe birds evolved from what group of animals about 150 million years ago?

Dinosaurs.

Feathers—birds are covered with them.
The snowy egret has a spiky crown of them.

Feathers and Wings

A bird's wings are covered with feathers. They are made of the same material as your fingernails. Most feathers grow out of little tubes in a bird's skin. If you look closely at chicken skin before it is cooked, you can see where the feathers once were on the bird's body.

Most birds have two kinds of feathers—**down feathers** and **contour feathers.** Short, fluffy down feathers are found underneath the contour feathers. Down feathers help keep a bird warm.

Contour feathers cover a bird's body, wings, and tail. The long contour feathers on a

A down feather.

In this close-up view of a snow goose's wing, you can see several contour feathers.

bird's wings are called flight feathers. They move a bird through the air. Tail feathers help a bird steer, slow down, and keep its balance. Shorter contour feathers cover the rest of a bird's body.

Now I Know!

How do down feathers help a bird?

They keep it warm.

All contour feathers have a stiff, hollow part in the center called the **shaft.** A flat **vane** is found on each side of the shaft. The vanes may look like one solid piece, but they are made up of hundreds of small, hairlike **barbs.** Branching out from each barb are even smaller **barbules.** Hundreds of tiny hooks hold each barbule together. They keep the air from flowing through the feather and allow a bird to fly.

A bird's body is designed to help it
move easily through the air.

The Perfect Body

Feathers and wings are not the only special body parts that help birds to fly. To take off and soar through the sky, a bird must overcome gravity. Gravity is an invisible force that pulls objects toward Earth. Gravity tugs hardest on heavy objects, so birds have developed many ways to lighten their load.

Hollow bones help make birds light enough to soar through the sky.

A bird's beak weighs very little. But it works just as well as the heavy jaws and teeth of other animals. A bird also has hollow bones and bubble-like air sacs inside its body. Even though a bald eagle has a large body and a 7-foot (2.1-meter) **wingspan,** it weighs only about 10 pounds (4.5 kilograms.)

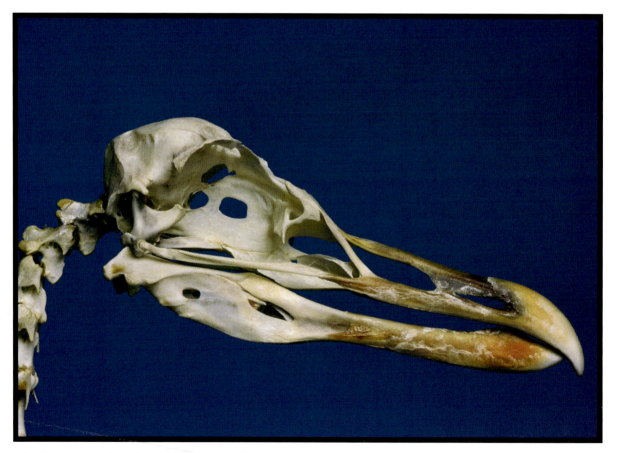

The bones in a herring gull's head and neck.

A group of birds passes in front of the Moon.

A bird's thin, light legs help it to be an efficient flier.

A bird has ears, even though you can't see them. They are inside its head. Not having ears on the outside of its body helps cut down on **wind resistance.** It is a force that slows objects as they move through the air. As most birds fly, they hold their slim legs close to their body. This also helps to reduce wind resistance. A bird's heaviest body parts are located in places that help it stay balanced as it flies. Together, these features help birds move through the air without using too much of the energy they get from food.

Now I Know!

Where are a bird's ears found?

Inside its head.

A Stellar's jay with a peanut in its beak.

Fueling Flight

Because flying uses up so much energy, a bird must eat more food than other animals its size. A kinglet eats about one-third of its body weight each day. If you weigh 100 pounds (45 kilograms), that would be like eating 120 quarter-pound hamburgers every day of your life!

An adult bittern feeds a frog to its hungry chicks.

Birds spend almost all their time looking for and eating the foods that will give them the energy they need. Woodpeckers and swallows eat insects, while robins usually search for earthworms. Chickadees eat nuts and seeds, while toucans and parrots prefer fruit. Hawks hunt for fish and small mammals, while vultures feed on creatures that are already dead.

A bird's **digestive system** helps it get energy from the food it eats. People take about a day to digest their meals. A bird's digestive system can do the same job in as little as thirty minutes.

After a bird breaks down food in its stomach and **gizzard,** the thick, soupy paste enters a narrow, twisting tube called the **small intestine.** Then **nutrients** from the food move into the blood and travel to **cells** all over the body.

At the same time, a gas called **oxygen** has been entering the bird's body. Every time a bird breathes in, some of the fresh air enters its lungs. Oxygen in the air passes into the bird's blood. The rest of the fresh air travels to special air sacs. They help to keep the bird's body cool.

When the bird breathes out, stale air leaves its lungs. Fresh

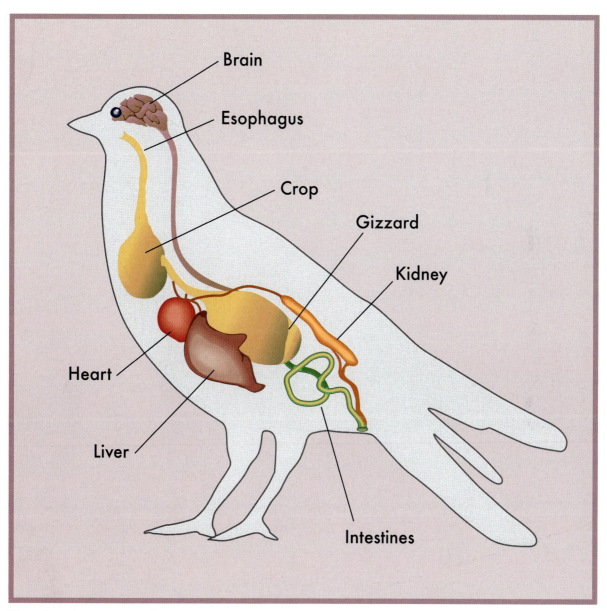

The digestive system of a bird. Food helps a bird get the energy it needs to soar through the sky.

Breathing in, breathing out, a chickadee takes a brief rest. Oxygen helps a bird burst into flight.

air, rich in oxygen, flows from the air sacs into the lungs. This means oxygen is always moving into a bird's blood vessels, so it can be sent to the cells very quickly.

Oxygen and the nutrients from food meet up inside a bird's cells. They then combine and give off the energy a bird needs to live, grow, and fly.

If a bird senses danger, it can break into flight in less than a second.

How Do Birds Fly?

Like an airplane, a bird must take off before it can cruise through the air. Most birds take off by jumping from their perch, spreading their wings, and flapping them up and down. As a bird moves through the air, the curved shape of its wings helps to lift the bird up.

As a bird raises its wings, feathers along the outer edge of the wings move apart and let some of the air slip through. This makes it easier for the bird to lift its wings through the

This series of photos shows how a Japanese crane takes off.

A hummingbird is a master flier. It moves its wings quickly and flits about in short, jerking movements.

air. When a bird lowers its wings, the feathers stay together. The force of the wing pressing against the air around it is what moves the bird forward.

To land, a bird stops flapping its wings and spreads them wide. Then it uses its tail to slow down and steer to a safe landing spot.

Each bird species flies in a slightly different way. After a little practice, you can learn to **identify** a bird by the size and shape of its wings and the way it moves them. Albatross spend most of their lives flying far and fast over open water. They have long, narrow wings with pointed tips. Pheasants live in forests. Their shorter, wider wings are perfect for flying short distances, taking off quickly, and weaving between trees. A bird's wings and style of flight help it survive in its habitat.

✸ Activity ✸

To understand how a bird flies, try this activity.

1. Cut a piece of paper about 2 inches (5 centimeters) wide and 6 inches (15 cm) long.

2. Hold one corner of the strip of paper between the thumb and first finger of each hand.

3. Blow over the top of the paper until the free end lifts up.

In this activity, the paper acts just like a bird's wings. Your breath is like the air birds fly through. As you blow over the top of the paper, air on the upper surface of the paper moves quickly. As the fast-flowing air moves, it pulls the paper up. The slower-moving air on the bottom surface also pushes up, helping to lift the paper.

🕊 Glossary 🕊

barb—A small part of a bird's feather that branches off the shaft.

barbule—A tiny part of a bird's feather that branches off a barb.

cell—The basic building block of all living things.

contour feather—One of the feathers that covers a bird's body, wings, and tail.

digestive system—The parts of the body involved in breaking down food and moving nutrients into the blood.

down feather—One of the soft, fluffy feathers that helps keep a bird warm.

evolve—To change over time.

gizzard—The part of a bird's digestive system that does the same job as the teeth of other animals.

gravity—An invisible force that pulls objects to Earth.

habitat—The place where a plant or animal lives.

identify—To know, name, or recognize.

migrate—To travel a long distance to find food or a place to mate and raise young.

nutrient—A substance that keeps the body of a living thing healthy.

oxygen—An invisible gas in the air. Animals need it to release energy from food.

reptile—An animal that lives on land, lays eggs, and is cold blooded. Examples include turtles, snakes, lizards, and alligators.

shaft—The hollow central part of a bird's feather.

small intestine—The part of the digestive system where nutrients pass into the blood.

species—A group of similar creatures that can mate and produce healthy young.

vane—The part of a bird's feather that branches off both sides of the shaft.

wind resistance—A force that slows objects as they travel through the air.

wingspan—The distance a bird can spread its wings from tip to tip.

Find Out More

BOOKS

Arnold, Caroline. *Birds: Nature's Magnificent Flying Machines.* Watertown, MA: Charlesbridge, 2003.

Brynie, Faith Hickman. *101 Questions about Food and Digestion That Have Been Eating at You—Until Now.* Brookfield, CT: Twenty-first Century Books, 2002.

Laubach, Christyna M. *Raptor! A Kid's Guide to Birds of Prey.* North Adams, MA: Storey Books, 2002.

Salmansohn, Pete, and Stephen W. Kress. *Saving Birds: Heroes around the World.* Gardiner, ME: Tilbury House, 2002.

Weidensaul, Scott. *National Audubon Society First Field Guide: Birds.* New York: Scholastic, 1998.

WEB SITES

The Bird Site
http://www.lam.mus.ca.us/birds/guide/pg018.html

How Does a Bird Fly?
http://yahooligans.yahoo.com/content/animals/birds/birds_howdotheyfly.html

 Index

Page numbers for illustrations are in **boldface.**